Actually Useful Self-Employment: How to Escape the Salary Trap

by Phil Cohen
Copyright 2013 Phil Cohen, all rights reserved.
ISBN: 149483071X
ISBN-13: 978-1494830717

Contents

Introduction 3

Enough is Enough 5

What's wrong with a salary? 7

First carefully fold your parachute 9

Options 15

Be a contractor 17

Buy a business 25

Partners 31

Set up your own business 35

Business courses 39

Business plans 41

Business structures 47

Taxes and licenses 49

You and your business 51

Get some support 55

It's not all gloom and doom 57

What's next? 59

Introduction

I made the transition to self-employment the easy way: I had no choice. I'd been fired twice out of my first four jobs and I was pretty sure being self-employed was the only way I was going to survive.

Not only did I survive: I thrived. I've worked as a freelancer, started and run several successful businesses and helped hundreds of others make the transition from salary to hourly rate, and from hourly rate to full self-employment.

This book tells you everything you need to start that journey, and to avoid some of the biggest traps along the way.

I make no secret of the fact that I'm risk-averse. I hope you are too. The job of this book is to get you from where you are now to where you'd like to be as safely as possible.

Phil Cohen, Sydney, 2013

All material copyright Phil Cohen, Sydney, 2013.

Enough is Enough

This is a book for people who've had enough. Enough of earning a mediocre salary while others are earning more. Enough of putting up with dull bosses. Enough of waiting for the weekend, for holidays, even for sick days, so they can escape a job they're not inspired by. Enough of wondering what they could achieve if they were in charge of their own business.

Leaving regular paid employment is just like stepping off a cliff. That first step is a scary one ... which is why most people never take it. But everyone who takes that step with proper preparation will soar to new heights.

This book will run through your pre-flight checks, and help you build confidence so that you take that first step. It's a step I took myself in 1984, and one which I've helped hundreds of others take since.

What's wrong with a salary?

Maybe nothing.

If you can answer 'yes' to all of these questions, then there's no reason for you to change:

- Every Sunday I look forward to Monday mornings
- I contribute all that I am capable of at work
- What makes my job difficult also makes it interesting and exciting
- When I have a work task to perform, I can do it in whatever way I think best
- There is no end to what I can achieve at work
- I don't think I'll ever want to retire
- I tell people I enjoy my job … and they believe me
- I only ever get sick at weekends
- People I went to school with tell me they wish they'd made the work choices I did

Think about what your life would be like if you could answer 'yes' to *all* of these questions.

This book is about one thing: how to get out from under your current job, if that's what you need to do. And if you make the right choice now, then very soon you'll be able to answer yes to all of the questions above.

Organisations are built as hierarchies, with each person getting their instruction and motivation from the person above them. Even right at the top, company directors have to answer to shareholders, and senior public servants have to report to a politician. We're all trapped in this sticky web of trickle-down instruction.

This sometimes means that you're trapped next to someone who you find difficult to work with. At the very least it means that your freedom to do things your own way is restricted. That's the way large organisations work most of the time.

But what if you could move to a situation where you answer only to ... yourself. The owners of small businesses don't have to answer to anyone - not bosses, not shareholders, and not politicians. There are no rules other than the ones you make up for yourself. You can build the business as large as you like, and the only limit is yourself and your capabilities.

That's not to say that there are no stresses working for yourself: there are. But they are stresses that make your work life more interesting. There are risks, but they are risks you can control - and you get the returns for facing those risks.

The hard part is taking that first step - stepping off that cliff of full-time employment into the clear air of working for yourself. But having taken that step, you'll find that the journey is an exhilarating one, and nowhere near as risky as you might think.

First carefully fold your parachute

Before you start, there's one thing you have to get in place: your parachute. If you jump off the cliff and want to change your mind, it would be nice to have some way of getting back into a full-time job if you need to.

Now, this isn't one of these "have faith and everything will fall in your lap" books. Some authors will try to tell you that if you believe strongly enough in something, or have a positive enough attitude, then all will be well. I don't subscribe to that theory. I've seen enough people fail in business to know that it's not risk-free. But I can also tell you how to make those risks survivable so you can try again later if you need to. And keep trying till you do succeed.

When you leave a room, do you ever turn around and tell everyone in it what you think of them, and then say that you'd rather eat your own hand than come back into that room? Doesn't sound like a good idea to do that ... particularly if you later want to come back into the room to get your coat/phone/baby.

And yet that's what some people do when they leave full-time employment. They let the pressures build up until they can't take it any more, than unload on their boss and co-workers. It just comes out.

Now think what happens when they try to get into another full-time job. First, they're unemployed (and employers don't like to hire people who've been unemployed for any length of time, given the choice). Second, they certainly can't reapply for their old job. And third they can't give their former employer as a reference.

So don't wait until the frustrations with your current job have taken you to the edge of going postal. Make plans now, and calmly put them into place, so that you can exit from your current employment and get back in (or at least, into another job) if you need to later.

Imagine for a moment you're hiring new staff and you're presented with three applicants:

- Applicant one is currently employed with a competitor, and would need to give four weeks' notice before they could come and work for you.

- Applicant two has been unemployed for six months, and left their previous job suddenly.

- Applicant three has spent the past six months trying to start their own business, and before that gave plenty of notice to their employer. The business didn't work out, so now they want to get back into the workforce.

Applicant three would be my preference (and I've hired more than a few people in my time). Applicant one can't start for four weeks (and no-one starts hiring unless they need someone right away, so I'd rather have someone who could start sooner rather than later). Applicant two looks like they have had problems in their previous job; when I ask them for a referee at their previous employer they say that they left because of a 'personality clash': not a good look.

But applicant three looks like they have their act together. They left their previous employer on good terms, to do something that shows they have initiative (which for any intelligent employer is a positive attribute). They've tried it, presumably got it out of their system, and now they want to get back into a job.

So before you jump off the cliff, build your parachute. If your boss is complaining about your timekeeping, or your level of work, or whatever, start fixing that. Make sure that when you do leave, you can give them as a referee in case you need one.

Before you leave:

Give more notice than your employment contract asks for - tell your employer that you want to make sure they have time to find a replacement before you go.

Tell your employer why you're leaving: you're going to start your own business. You might even tell them that you're going to try it for six months and see what happens ... they may even offer you your old job back (if you need it).

Let your annual leave build up, and ask for it to be paid when you go (most employment contracts and legislation will let you do this); that way you'll have the maximum amount of cash available when you start - and all you've given up is a holiday.

Ask for a written reference. This is considered old-fashioned, and any potential employer will still call your previous one for a verbal reference. But the advantage is that, having given you a good written reference, it will be harder for them to give you a bad verbal one.

Make sure you're on good terms with your boss, and with everyone else you work with. If this is too hard, just focus on your boss.

There are some other things you can do as well, that will help you succeed in your new enterprise:

Take whatever training is going, particularly if you think it will help when you're out on your own. And even more particularly sales training.

Start going to conferences and other meetings where you might meet people who will be your eventual customers when you do leave. Keep records of the people you meet. Your current employment contract may have a clause in it that says you can't compete with your current employer after you leave, but there's no reason you can't make useful contacts for business that doesn't compete - including customers of your current employer. So if for example you're working for an IT company and you want to go into business selling flowers, there is probably nothing stopping you from keeping records of the people you meet in IT who might also want to buy flowers later.

When you leave, make sure that you visit as many people as you can in your current employment and tell them what you'll be doing once you leave.

To make sure that you can survive until your new source of income starts paying, you'll also have to think about saving more than you normally would (or arranging to borrow, although that shouldn't be your first choice). How much you'll need will depend on which of the options in this book you take up, but you should start saving while you're still in full-time employment.

If you're a cautious person (and I have to admit that I am) then you will be tempted to take all of the advice I've given in this chapter and keep preparing until you're old enough to retire. Don't make that mistake: the purpose of preparation is action, not more preparation.

Give yourself a deadline: will it take six months for you to prepare properly? Or a year? Or a week? Set a date and work backwards from it to the day you give your notice, and then stick to that. Tell your partner and your friends what you intend to do, so that it's harder to back out of if you get cold feet later.

Prepare by all means, but also act.

Options

There are many options open to you, and the one you choose will depend on what you want to get out of the process.

The ones that I'll look at in this book are:

- working as an hourly- or daily-rate contractor through recruitment companies and consulting firms
- buying a business
- starting your own business

Remember that none of these is a one-way street. You can start your own business, decide that's not for you and work as a contractor, then buy a business, and then get back into full-time employment. Or any combination you choose. After all, this is about your own personal freedom.

I suggest you read the rest of this book before you make any decisions about which way to go.

Be a contractor

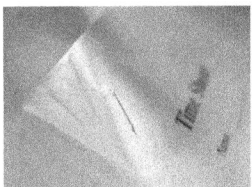

Contract staff are most common in a number of industries that are based around projects, like IT and engineering. The structure of those industries means that employers need numbers of specialist staff for specific periods, and the most flexible way of doing this is to hire people by the hour or by the day. Of course, IT and engineering firms have permanent staff as well, but they supplement these with contractors.

If the work that you do has nothing to do with projects, don't worry. Contractors are commonly used for many other specialist jobs including everything from nursing to book editing. Before you decide to become a contractor, you should of course make sure that there will be a market for your services. The best way to find out is to use job search web site - if there are fixed-term contracts available for something that you can offer, then there's a market.

There are a number of ways you can get work as a contractor. You can go 'direct' to an employer, or you can contract through a recruitment agency, or you can work for a consulting firm that hires contractors.

In those scenarios, at the end of each week you'll complete a timesheet showing when you worked, get it signed by your employer, and you will be paid for the time you worked.

Many contractors stay with the same employer for long periods, and put in the same number of hours each week. Sounds familiar? If you're not careful, then being a contractor can be just another name for being salaried - but with differences.

For one thing, you'll get paid more. Because of the risk inherent in contracting (which I'll come to in a minute) you should get a minimum of 25% more per hour than you would as an employee. That's a minimum - in most cases you should get considerably more.

The downsides of contracting include the fact that you don't get holiday or sick pay. If you don't show up for work, you don't get paid. Period. That introduces certain risks, as well as reducing the effective rate that you're paid (after all, everyone gets sick and needs a break from time to time).

If you're going to be a contractor, you'll need insurance to cover you when you're sick. Depending on what country you live in, you may also need health insurance. (Most non-US countries have automatic health cover provided by the Government, even when you're not working).

Another problem is that you can be laid off at short notice (sometimes, depending on your contract, at no notice at all). Of course, salaried employees are laid off as well, but it's easier to lay off contractors.

Most contracts run for between a week and six months; governments are large users of contract labour and many have a maximum period that they can hire contractors for (in Australia it's about three months), so you often find contractors who are on a series of three-month contracts with the same employer, sometimes for years.

Another advantage of contracting is that you can renegotiate your hourly or daily rate towards the end of each contract period. If they hire you for three months, then at the end of that time all bets are off. You can leave if you want to (it's not like quitting a full-time job, because you only ever agreed to work for those three months), and you can ask for a raise for the following three months. Of course, they can always say no, but it's a more straightforward arrangement than the complex loyalties that staff and employer owe each other in full-time employment.

You'll find that working as a contractor makes your job feel different, too. The people you work with (particularly if they're salaried) will be conscious of the fact that you're paid by the hour, and they will be less inclined to waste your time as a result - after all, that would mean they're wasting their employer's money.

Sometimes you'll meet jealousy from permanent employees because you're paid more than they are. If you do, give them a copy of this book.

Your employability as a contractor will depend on a number of things, and one of them will be your reputation. Some things you should never do as a contractor include:

- trying to renegotiate your contract in the middle of it

- leaving a contract without completing it (for *any* reason)

- putting down hours on your timesheet that you haven't worked

- turning up late for work, even if you reflect that on your timesheet

- falling out with people

- not being able to do the work you've contracted to do

If you're good at what you do, and stick to the rules about contracting, it can be a very refreshing way to work. You can change jobs every few months without people thinking there's a problem with you: if variety is what you're after, this might be the answer. Over the years you'll build up a picture of your whole industry.

You can find work as a contractor by approaching potential employers directly, or by going through a recruitment company.

Recruitment companies that deal with contractors (not all of them do) will write two contracts: one with you, and one with your actual contract employer. They'll pay you, and invoice your employer, for each timesheet that you present. The difference between what they pay you and what they charge is their margin. Margins range from a few percent to tens of percent: but that shouldn't matter to you, because your rate will be negotiated between you and the recruitment company; you may never know what they're actually charging for you (although it's valuable information which you should find out if you can!).

Consulting firms also use contractors, and in fact there is precious little difference between a consulting firm and a recruiting firm (I should know, I've run both), except that the consulting firm charges more and takes responsibility for its customer's outcomes.

The most important thing to remember about being a contractor, whether you get work direct, through a recruiter or through a consulting firm, is that *everything* is negotiable. Your daily rate, how often you work, whether you get paid for travel time, whether you can claim expenses ... everything. But it's only negotiable until you sign a contract, then it's fixed for the duration of that contract.

If you're good at negotiating, and good at your job, you can make a lot of money contracting. I know dozens of people who have been contractors for years or decades, and would never want to work any other way. I've worked as a contractor myself and thoroughly enjoyed it. For me, the best part was being able to change employers regularly without my resume looking flakey because of multiple short job durations.

If you approach a recruitment company, remember that despite what they tell you, your rate is up to you, not to them. Recruiters can make more money by talking down the contractor's rate and talking up the client's rate up, so when they tell you that the client "has a fixed budget" or that "the market won't pay any more than x" remember that you can always say no. But of course, so can they.

Generally more 'professional' engagements will be paid on a daily rate and more 'technical' engagements will be on an hourly rate.

What does a daily rate mean? If you get in to work at 10am and leave a 3pm is that a day? If you have to work till 10pm is that still a day? Generally employers will try to get you on a daily rate if they think that the type of work will involve you working long hours - it's essentially telling you that you don't get paid for overtime. But you can insist (remember: *everything's* negotiable) on a higher daily rate to compensate for that, or you can insist on an hourly rate instead.

Watch out for payment delays. Ask the agency/consulting firm when you will get paid. Often they will try to pay you as late as possible (so that they've got the client's money before they have to pay you) but ... yes, it's negotiable. The very best agencies will pay you on the same day that you submit your timesheet; a week later is pretty good. End of the month is acceptable, but end of the following month is not. The earlier you get paid, the better.

If someone says that they'll pay you on a certain date, and then don't make the payment, that's a big red flag. If the recruitment company or consulting firm is small, and they start making excuses like "you just missed this week's pay run" or "one of our signatories is overseas" then you need to think very carefully about whether you will ever be paid. Tell them that you need the cash urgently to pay your rent (or whatever) - they will know that desperate people do desperate things (like break their contract).

Contracting is definitely more fun than regular salaried employment, but it does have its risks. What you'll find is that you won't be working all year - there will inevitably be gaps between your engagements, and you won't be paid during those gaps. That's one of the reasons why you'll need at least 25% more per hour than your regular salary.

But that doesn't mean you'll get long holidays. In fact, you may get no holidays at all. It works like this: you're given two months work, and during that time you really can't (nor would you want to) take a break. After all, there's money to be made and if you take a week off you don't get paid for it. As your contract starts coming to an end, you'll be looking for your next assignment - and you hope it will start right after your current one ends. If it doesn't, you'll be approaching recruitment companies or potential employers and won't let up until you find your next contract.

Pretty much the only way you can arrange a holiday is to schedule it months in advance, and every time you go talk to a recruitment company or employer, tell them that if they hire you for this contract it will be on the basis that they give you the time off for your scheduled holiday. As long as that suits their schedule they won't have a problem with that.

However, they say that a change is as good as a holiday, and although I seldom took breaks when I was a contractor, I never felt the need for them either.

Once you're a settled and successful contractor, you may be quite happy to stay that way for the rest of your working life. I know plenty of people who have. But on the other hand, it might not be enough for you.

That's the realisation I came to: there are only so many working hours in the week, and you can only charge so much per hour. If you want more, you have to run a business.

Buy a business

The easiest way to get into business is to buy one. It's also the easiest way to go broke. After all, buying a business is not like buying a car; you can't take the business back if it doesn't run at a profit.

There are thousands of franchises available, and they're pretty easy to buy into. Some of them may be right for you, but many of them are death traps. In most Western countries there are sets of laws that give some protection to franchisees (people who buy franchises). Those laws are there for a reason: because it's really easy for the franchisor (the person who's selling the franchise) to rip you off.

The ideal franchise arrangement from a franchisor's point of view is one that takes all of your commercial freedom and almost all of your profit, and leaves you with what's essentially a salaried job and a huge debt. Some franchise contracts will say that you can only buy goods or services from the franchisor, but allow them to arbitrarily increase the price of those goods and services. Some will insist that they own the lease on the land or buildings that the franchise sits on. Some give them the right to take money out of the business' bank account whenever they like. Sounds unreasonable? It is, but it happens.

Many of the advantages of owning a franchise are also disadvantages. The fact that you have the right to use a recognised brand sounds like a plus, but it also means that you're helping build a brand that you don't own: at the end of the day it's still the franchisor's brand, not yours.

The fact that they provide operating procedures and training sounds like a plus, but it also limits your opportunity to innovate, and to build a business that you create from your own imagination.

The fact that they will do all of the marketing and advertising sounds like a plus, but again they're advertising their brand not yours, and passing out the leads that come in gives them a lot of power over you.

I'm not saying you shouldn't buy a franchise. But do your homework: ask a specialist franchise lawyer that you trust to check any contracts. Talk to lots of franchisees, and track down some ex-franchisees to see what they think as well. After all, the last thing you want to do with your savings is to buy what is effectively a salaried job with long hours, no security and no overtime pay.

Of course, buying a business doesn't always mean buying into a franchise. There are plenty of small businesses for sale that aren't franchises. There are people called business brokers who (like real estate brokers) help people buy and sell small businesses of any type.

Before you buy a business you have to ask yourself a very important question: can I run this business? Talk to the business owner and ask them what skills and knowledge they have that helps them run their business: ask yourself whether you already have (or could pick up) that knowledge.

You'll also need to figure out if the business is profitable, or at least if you could make it profitable. Ask to see at least the last three years' financial statements (preferably five years). If you can't read a Profit and Loss statement buy my book "Actually Useful Accounting". Ask to see a statement from the tax authorities that shows all of the taxes are paid up to date.

Some more homework: go talk to the customers of the business and see what they think about it. Talk to the major suppliers. Talk to the staff (you'll have to work with them, and them with you). Find some ex staff and talk to them. Talk to the business' competitors. Talk to some ex customers as well, find out why they're ex and what it would take to make them come back.

There's an old saying "sin in haste, repent at leisure". If you buy a business and make it work, you're going to be running it for a long time. If you buy a dud it's going to be a long time before you have the money to try again. So take your time, check everything out and make sure you're happy with it all. No-one will fault you for your diligence, even if the current owner and the business broker keep telling you that they have another buyer offering more just around the corner. There are plenty more businesses for sale.

Of course, not everything you find will be squeaky clean. It' will be up to you to decide what's relevant. Every business has disgruntled employees, or upset ex customers.

At this point it's worth knowing something about how people (specifically: you) buy things. There's a sales saying: people buy on emotion, reject with logic. What that means is this: when you look at a business it's all too easy to think of yourself running it, and how nice that would be. You might think of the reputation you'll have among your friends and relatives as a business owner, or about what you will say to your ex-boss. Or that owning a business will make you happy. All of these things might be true, but you have to put them to one side when you're actually making the decision about what business to buy.

Actually: you should put emotion to one side every time you make a major purchase.

Think about the last time you bought a house, or a second-hand car. Were there any things you wish you'd thought to ask (or to check) before you made that purchase? Often your emotion - the almost physical need to be in that house, or to be driving that car - will get in the way of your decision-making.

Be particularly careful in choosing a business. Buying a dud car, or a dud house, can cause you headaches certainly. But buying a dud business can ruin your life properly.

Having said all of that, if you've checked the business out and it seems profitable (but not suspiciously so), and you reckon you can run it, and all of the other things you've checked have all panned out, there's one more question you have to ask yourself: could you build this business from scratch using just the money that they're asking for it? In other words, if you took the money you're about to spend on buying this business and put it into your own brand-new business, would you be better off or worse off?

Remember that when you're no longer an employee, everything is negotiable. This applies even more strongly to the process of buying a business as it does to working as a contractor. Think about what you could ask for that would reduce your costs, or your risks, in the new business. For example, you could ask that part of the price you pay will be a percentage of the profit of the business as you run it during the first year. Or you could ask for the current owner to work beside you in the business for three months to train you. Or ... well anything, really. The worst that can happen is that the seller says no.

The business broker will try to convince you that you're being unreasonable: but they would, wouldn't they? And after all, it's your money.

You'll need to hire a lawyer for the detailed process of buying the business. There should be a formal contract which includes all of the things you've agreed with the seller. Even if the business broker comes up with a contract, hire a lawyer to check it for you. Unfortunately some things are just unavoidable, and (all due respect to my lawyer: sorry, T!) lawyers are one of them!

Buying a business for the first time is going to be one of the most challenging things that you've ever done in your life. But - despite the fact that I've just spent several pages telling you all of the things that can go wrong! - it's not all negative. Owning a healthy business is one of the most satisfying and liberating things you can do with your life. Get it right, and you'll never regret it.

Partners

Whether you buy a business or set up a new one, you'll be tempted to involve one or more partners. After all, you're moving into brand new territory where you'd really appreciate some moral and logistical support. Choose carefully.

If your (life) partner becomes your business partner, any stresses you meet in your new business will make themselves felt in your relationship. If your relationship is rock solid, that probably won't be a problem. Just saying.

With any partner it's important to have some ground rules: not all decisions can be made by all partners, so there should be some division of labour around decision-making. In my business I look after consulting and training delivery, and my business partner looks after sales. We still disagree on things that affect both delivery and sales, but at least we know where our relative strengths lie.

In some households it's agreed who does the shopping and who does the gardening, and both of them get done without any problems. In other households there are constant arguments about whose turn it is to shop, and what sort of plants to put in. Same with a business partnership: split the work between you equitably and let the other person get on with it.

It's also worth having a conversation about what you and your partner(s) want to get out of the business. That's pretty fundamental: different people go into business for different reasons, and it's important to at least know what the other partners' reasons are, even if you don't totally agree with them.

For example, some people go into business so that they can take money out and spend it, over and above what they need to live on As long as the business is making money, that's not a problem.

Other people want to build the business up so they can sell it and make a capital gain. No problem with that either, except that it clashes with the idea of taking money out: if you want to build the business as quickly as possible you might want to reinvest that money in the business instead, and take out only enough to live on.

Some people want to run the business because they enjoy the work, and don't really care too much about the money as long as they get to do what they enjoy.

Others want the responsibility of controlling a business, regardless of anything else. You can call them a control freak if you like, but it's their choice.

Some even want to run a business for the good of the community - people who run not-for-profit businesses have this aim (well, most of them do).

Some people start their own business because they're been fired once too many times.

I'm sure there are many more reasons why people go into business for themselves. The point I'm making is that if you want to take on partners, you should have a discussion with them about your and their reasons for going into business. If you have completely different (and perhaps conflicting) reasons then you shouldn't be partners.

A used car salesman once told me that he often had people approach him to see if they could buy a car and be issued a false receipt. Not so they could fool the tax man (although that happened too) but so they could fool their business partner. His advice was: don't ever take on a business partner. Goes without saying that trust is also a vital part of any partnership: be absolutely sure that anyone you are going to partner is someone you would trust with your credit cards.

Set up your own business

One of the decisions you should make before you buy a business is this: could I set up on my own? And if I did, would that be better than buying someone else's business?

Of course, the advantage of buying a business is that (in theory at least) it's already up and running and you know it's going to work. Whereas with your own, you really have no idea whether it will be successful or not.

But then again, if you can't afford to buy a business, or can't find one that you think would suit you, then you'll be better off starting your own. And if you do it right, you might not need a lot of capital to start with.

Perhaps you could start by taking a few contract positions to build up both your experience and also your capital. Or you could just start your business low-key (even part-time while you're still working for someone else).

The safest way to start a new business is: slowly. Any new business is a risk, and you can reduce that risk by taking baby steps. One of the things you'll find when you start a business is that the business you start is not the one that you end up with.

For example, let's say that you start a pet walking business. You put fliers round your neighbourhood telling people you'll walk their dogs for them. Maybe that doesn't work, and you realise that the people where you live like to walk their own dogs: so you try a richer neighbourhood. That works, but you find that your customers also ask if you can wash their dogs once a week as well. You find that there's more money in dog washing than dog walking, so you end up with a (related but) different business in a different geography than you started with. The business you **build** is always different to the business you **start**.

This story is not unusual. The first business I started was technical copywriting, but that didn't go anywhere so we started doing technical public relations instead. Then I realised that there was more money in technical writing (user manuals, etc) so we dropped the PR work and focussed on writing manuals.

This is not an unusual story, and when you start a business you'll often find that the demand from your customers will drag you in a direction that you didn't think of. The moral is this: if you put a huge amount of resources into the business that you **start**, you may well get into trouble. But if you start slow, find out what your customers will actually buy, and then put in the resources, you'll avoid that trap.

There are two things that kill businesses stone dead: optimism and cash flow. Optimism makes people keep thrashing the business they start, and ignoring the signs that they need to a) give up gracefully and start again another day or b) change their business so it meets the actual demand.

Cash flow problems are due to inexperience: they often come from expecting customers to pay you when they say they're going to pay you. Guess that's partly optimism as well.

So: find a way to start your business slowly. If you want to buy a cake oven and make cakes in bulk, maybe you can rent space in someone else's oven to start with, then buy your own when you know the demand is there.

Certainly if you want to start a business that doesn't require any massive equipment or capital outlay, you should start small (Maybe just you? Maybe even just you part time?). After all, when you learn to drive you don't go out and buy a car, then get in it and take off at full speed. Running a business needs knowledge, and the best (in fact, the only) way to get that knowledge is by doing the job. Inevitably you're going to make mistakes - so make sure that the mistakes you make are small by starting small.

Business courses

There are some things you can learn about business from academics. I did an MBA about 20 years ago, when I'd already been running my business for 10 years, and there were some things that I learned from that MBA that have been very useful. Perhaps 10% of the courses I took were useful; the other 90% were fascinating, but a waste of time.

The two key things that I learned from my MBA were a) double-entry bookkeeping (which you can learn from one of my books) and b) that no-one else knows anything about management either.

Apart from accounting, the other very useful course was in business law. Other than that, there wasn't much of actual use for a small business. Finance is all very well if you're going to go into banking, but subjects like communication and organisational behaviour (OB) are pretty much a waste of time. (My OB lecturer told me that OB theories were 'contingent', by which he meant that a theory that worked in one workplace might not work anywhere else). Economics is fascinating but doesn't work.

So: by all means take some courses before you go into business. Certainly if there are courses or qualifications you need that relate directly to what you want to do ("Introductory dog grooming") then go for it. And accounting and a bit of law are always useful. But don't get sucked it by your local university or college telling you that they can teach you how to run a business: they can't.

The ineffective "entrepreneurship' course that was part of my MBA was taught by an academic whose claim to fame was that he started a consulting firm with two other academics that they ran part-time while still lecturing, and failed.

One place you can go to find out more about business is a networking organisation, or some other place where you can meet other people who are starting, or running, small businesses. The vast majority of them won't be competing with you, and will be delighted to share their experience and insights with you. A one-hour conversation over coffee with someone in a related business will be of more value to you than a week spent being lectured to by an academic.

Business plans

Business academics make a big deal of business plans: there are dozens of business plan templates on the net, and to my mind, none of them is worth anything. There are two things that you need to develop before you start a business: collateral and a cash flow model.

Collateral: Back in the early days of B-grade movies, studios would commission an artist to work on a poster for a new move - before the script, or even the storyline had been written! The idea was that if they could come up with a poster that would make people show up at the movie, they could work the rest out later.

Science fiction publishers did the same thing: they commissioned book covers, and then picked one they liked and got an author to write a story behind it. After all, people do judge a book by its cover.

So when you start a business, the first thing you need to do is to work out what you think people will buy, and why. Put that into an email, or a flier, or poster, or whatever (the format will depend who you're selling to) and try it out. Change it depending on the feedback you get. When you have some collateral that you can show to someone and they say "hey, I'll buy that" then you have half of your business plan; all you have to do from there is to figure out how you're going to sell, and to deliver what you've got in your collateral.

Cash flow model: A cash flow model is generally built using a spreadsheet. The columns will represent the first 12 months of your business (or the first 20 weeks - we'll get back to that later), and the rows will represent ways money will come into or out of your business: - wages, sales, etc.

If you're good with a spreadsheet, then do this yourself. If you have no idea, find someone who knows how to use one and work with them instead.

Before we go on, I need to explain **accrual** accounting.

There are two ways of measuring money in a business: the 'cash method' and the 'accrual method'. In the cash method you measure cash when it leaves or arrives in your bank account. Sounds simple, right? Why would you measure it any other way?

Well let's say that your customers don't generally pay you right away, but after - say - a month. When you make a sale, the cash method shows the cash coming in a month later (when the customer actually pays). But the accrual method measures when the money is owed to you, rather than when it's paid. So the accrual method would count the income on the day the customer bought from you, rather than on the day they paid.

Why is this important? Well accruals actually let you measure profitability. If you spend a lot of money in January, and make a lot of sales in January, did you make money in January? The cash method would say 'no' because the sales might not result in actual cash until February. The accrual method would say 'yes'.

So the accrual method shows whether you made money or not, but the cash method shows whether you can actually pay your bills. In practice you need to use both to run (or to model) a business.

First, build your spreadsheet using the accrual method. I generally start by putting in a row that shows the number of sales staff (generally at the start this will be 1 - yourself). Then I show the level of sales (on an accrual basis) that those sales staff will generate.

```
                          Jan     Feb     Mar     Apr     May ...
1: sales staff              1       1       1       1       1
2: sales (row 1 x $6K)  $6,000  $6,000  $6,000  $6,000  $6,000
```

Below that I'll put the costs - first fixed costs like salaries and rent. Then 'variable' costs like raw materials and external contractor payments.

```
___$600____$600
                          Jan     Feb     Mar     Apr     May ...
1: sales staff              1       1       1       1       1
2: sales (row 1 x $6K)  $6,000  $6,000  $6,000  $6,000  $6,000
3: salary (row 1 x $2K) $2,000  $2,000  $2,000  $2,000  $2,000
4: rent                   $500    $500    $500    $500    $500
5: materials (row 2 / 10) $600   $600    $600    $600    $600
```

Now you can work out the profit month by month ("sales less costs").

```
                          Jan     Feb     Mar     Apr     May ...
1: sales staff              1       1       1       1       1
2: sales (row 1 x $6K)  $6,000  $6,000  $6,000  $6,000  $6,000
3: salary (row 1 x $2K) $2,000  $2,000  $2,000  $2,000  $2,000
4: rent                   $500    $500    $500    $500    $500
5: materials (row 2 / 10) $600   $600    $600    $600    $600
6: sales less costs     $2,900  $2,900  $2,900  $2,900  $2,900
```

But notice that this is an accrual measure for profit. You'll need to work out the cash flow *as well*. To do this, make an assumption about how long it will take your customers to actually pay you (I usually assume two months, which is slightly pessimistic) and use this to shift the sales to the right so that it represents cash actually coming in ("cash in").

	Jan	Feb	Mar	Apr	May ...
1: sales staff	1	1	1	1	1
2: sales (row 1 x $6K)	$6,000	$6,000	$6,000	$6,000	$6,000
3: salary (row 1 x $2K)	$2,000	$2,000	$2,000	$2,000	$2,000
4: rent	$500	$500	$500	$500	$500
5: materials (row 2 / 10)	$600	$600	$600	$600	$600
6: sales less costs	$2,900	$2,900	$2,900	$2,900	$2,900
7: cash in			$6,000	$6,000	$6,000

Then you can work out the 'cash flow' for each month by subtracting the costs (which you pay on the day) from the cash coming in. This gives a figure that goes positive or negative depending on whether your bank balance will go up or down that month.

	Jan	Feb	Mar	Apr	May ...
1: sales staff	1	1	1	1	1
2: sales (row 1 x $6K)	$6,000	$6,000	$6,000	$6,000	$6,000
3: salary (row 1 x $2K)	$2,000	$2,000	$2,000	$2,000	$2,000
4: rent	$500	$500	$500	$500	$500
5: materials (row 2 / 10)	$600	$600	$600	$600	$600
6: sales less costs	$2,900	$2,900	$2,900	$2,900	$2,900
7: cash in			$6,000	$6,000	$6,000
8: cash flow	-$3,100	-$3,100	$2,900	$2,900	$2,900

Finally you can total the cash flow to get a 'cumulative cash flow' figure which tells you how much capital you're going to need to get this thing going.

Then you can put in your initial bank balance (the amount of cash you'll need at the start before you launch this business) and it will tell you what your bank balance will be each month. Here (below) we start with $10,000 in December, drop to $3800 in February and we're up at $12,500 by May.

```
                         Jan       Feb       Mar       Apr       May ...
1: sales staff             1         1         1         1         1
2: sales (row 1 x $6K)  $6,000    $6,000    $6,000    $6,000    $6,000
3: salary (row 1 x $2K) $2,000    $2,000    $2,000    $2,000    $2,000
4: rent                   $500      $500      $500      $500      $500
5: materials (row 2 / 10) $600      $600      $600      $600      $600
6: sales less costs     $2,900    $2,900    $2,900    $2,900    $2,900
7: cash in                                   $6,000    $6,000    $6,000
8: cash flow           -$3,100   -$3,100    $2,900    $2,900    $2,900
9: cum cash flow       -$3,100   -$6,200   -$3,300     -$400    $2,500
10: bank balance        $6,900    $3,800    $6,700    $9,600   $12,500
```

If your bank balance goes negative, that means you either have to a) make sure you have an overdraft facility that can handle that b) put in more money to start with or c) start smaller.

A couple of things about these cash flow models.

First, the easiest part of the model to calculate accurately are the costs. I've seen cash flow models that have 50 rows of detail on the costs, and they're calculated to the nearest cent. But the line that is most critical? That's the sales.

If you get the costs wrong by 30% it probably won't do any harm. But if you get the sales wrong by 30% it almost certainly will. So what can you do about that? All you can do is to be conservative: make sure that your model shows something close to a worst-case, and then the worst that can happen is that you're pleasantly surprised.

The other thing about cash flow models is that they are never static. The additional 'funding' (ie money in the bank) that you need to start the business will also be needed every time the business grows. In the model above, what happens when you increase your sales staff from 1 to 2? Your salaries go up immediately, but the additional sales take time to come in as cash, so you'll need money in the bank before you hire that second person.

Other business plan elements: I've seen business plans that go on for pages, but unless you enjoy writing them, those two elements (a cash flow model and some collateral) are the only bits that are essential.

Yes, you can have pages explaining your marketing strategy, or your hiring strategy, or your social media approach, but at the end of the day all you need for a business is something to sell, a way to deliver it, and enough cash to get things moving without going broke.

Business structures

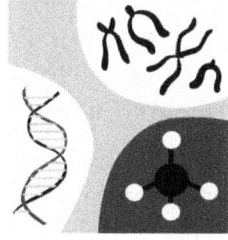
There are a variety of different legal structures you can use to build your business, and I'm not going to give you advice on this, because they vary from country to country. Depending on how big a business you are going to set up, you may or may not need to talk to a lawyer.

A good place to start is with the government. They generally have one department or another whose job it is to stimulate the growth of small businesses, and there may well be some useful information on their web site.

It can be a bit bewildering choosing between different legal entities: should you form a partnership, or just operate as a sole trader? Perhaps a limited liability company?

The factors you should think about are:

- **Risk** of going broke or getting sued: If you're very risk averse, or your business is inherently risky, you may want to choose a legal form that protects you as an individual even if the business goes under

- **Look and feel**: More formal business structures (such as limited liability companies) look more impressive to customers

- Running **cost**: Every company costs money to run - typically you'll pay an accountant to do your tax returns (at a minimum); some types of entity are more expensive to run than others

- Ease of **expansion**: How easy will it be to bring in partners later - for example, will it just be a case of selling them some shares? Or will it be more complicated?

- Ease of **credit**: Some suppliers will prefer a particular type of entity (say a limited company) when they're deciding whether to give you credit; some banks are the same

Just another word about risk. Although your limited liability company may provide protection to you as an individual shareholder or director if it goes under, you may find that in order to get a bank loan you'll have to sign an individual guarantee that waives that protection in the case of this particular loan. There are also laws that make directors personally responsible for some of the things that a company does (trading while insolvent, criminal acts, etc) so just bear this in mind when you're trading risk against cost. (You can find out what 'trading while insolvent' is by reading Actually Useful Accounting).

Taxes and licenses

Again, I can't give you advice on taxes and licenses that you might need because it varies from place to place, industry to industry, and time to time. But I can tell you that most state and national governments have lots of information available for small businesses: after all, they always want to you to have the correct licenses and pay the correct taxes. So just ask.

It's probably a good idea to look into this in some detail before you start, because it may be something you'll need to factor into your cash flow model. Find out when taxes are due, how they're calculated, and make sure that if the amount is significant you'll have enough money in the bank to pay it when it's due.

You and your business

One way of thinking about a business is as a separate legal entity. Something that has an existence separate from its owners or the people who work in it. In the case of a small business, this way of thinking about the business is **dead wrong, misleading and dangerous**.

As the owner/manager of a small business you'll find that there is essentially no difference between your mood and the 'mood' of the business. Between how your business is going and how you feel personally. Essentially you **are** the business and the business is **you**, despite what business theory tells you.

I spent the first several years in business noticing my mood swing from despondent ("I've delivered that project, but I have nothing left to deliver - need to go out and sell") to ecstatic ("I've just made a sale!"). Try to avoid letting the business drive your moods because you'll find it very hard to take in the long term.

Finally I started to notice that even when I wasn't expecting it, sales still happened. Slowly I stopped going up and down with the monthly sales figures and could keep myself on an even keel, even in the worst - and even more importantly in the best - months.

In a sense, problems with cash flow are due to: a) ignorance and b) optimism. We've solved (a) in the last few pages. But (b) may still be a problem. Make sure that when you estimate the cash that you need to keep in the black, you don't let any inherent optimism sway you. If you find yourself saying things like "I'm sure it will work out somehow", take a good step back and think about your mood. Optimism will kill your business stone dead if you let it.

So will pessimism. If you're so sure that you're not going to make a sale that you communicate that unconsciously to your customer, then you won't make that sale.

Successful small business owners come in two types: delusional people who think that they're doing fine no matter what, and people who've learned to distance themselves a little from the business and look at it dispassionately.

One of the worst things to happen to small business owners is the fad for 'positive thinking'. The idea is that as long as you retain a positive outlook, then good things will happen to you. Bull. Things will happen because you make them happen, or sometimes despite what you do. Being positive is a good thing if it helps you make sales, or motivate your staff, or stops you giving up, but on its own it won't make you successful. **You** have to do that.

One of the fundamental truths about any business is that sales is fundamental. Without sales, nothing else happens. Even if you build a better mousetrap, no-one will buy it if you don't have a good sales 'engine'.

There have been many many books written about sales, but the only one I can personally recommend (because I wrote it) is "Actually Useful B2B Selling". And that only deals with businesses that sell to other businesses.

If your business sells mainly to the public, don't buy that book because it won't work for you. If that's the case, I'd recommend doing some sales training. After all, you weren't allowed to drive on your own without being trained, and you're unlikely to be able to design a bridge without training, so what makes you think you can sell without training? Selling is harder than either bridge building (and I speak as a qualified engineer) or driving and will take you a lot longer to master.

I won't recommend a particular sales training course because there are so many of them. All of them are based on a single principle, though. It was formulated by Dale Carnegie, and published in a book he wrote titled "How to Win Friends and Influence People" in 1936. The principle is simply that people like to talk about themselves, and more you listen, the more they'll buy from you.

This principle is central to all of the sales methodologies that I've come across (about a dozen so far). But hang on, didn't I just say that sales was complicated and hard to master? Well it is - there's a lot more detail and a lot more technique that you'll have to learn and know how to apply before you're anywhere good at it, but that central principle still holds.

Other than that, sales training tends to be focussed on selling in a particular 'context'. So some courses are aimed at retail, some at B2B, some at winning work through tenders, some at selling over the phone, some at selling face to face. You'll need to choose a course that suits your business.

But unless you have done sales training before you start your business, I'd highly recommend that you do it now. If you're reading this book before you leave your 'day job', try getting your current employer to give you time off to do it.

Remember: nothing happens till you make a sale. And sales is something you have to learn.

Get some support

There are numerous organisations that exist only to help small businesses, but they are each useful for different things.

Every state, federal and national government has at least one department which is set up to support small business. They're useful for advice on what taxes to pay and what licenses you need. Sometimes they can help out with funding for training, which is useful.

There are many 'networking' organisations that let small business people get together and try to sell to each other. Depending on your business and your appetite for other people's pitches, you might find these of some value.

No matter what industry you're in, there will be an industry association. Join this, go to the meetings, and talk to as many people as you can. Even if they're your direct competitor, they are also the closest thing you have to a support network. Think siblings. I've always found it very valuable to be on good terms with my competitors: there is information that you can usefully swap with them (such as which clients don't pay, what's happening in the industry etc) that you just can't get anywhere else. If they're not immediately friendly to a newcomer remember Dale Carnegie: ask them about themselves and just keep listening.

There are other kinds of support groups for small business, some run as 'circles' without a leader, some with a professional coach or counsellor. Remember what I said about the difference between you and your business (ie that there is none)? Well, having someone work with you to figure out how your moods and your ideals interact with your business can be very valuable. And doing that in a group of your peers - people who have the same problems and the same opportunities - can be even more powerful.

It's not all gloom and doom

I've spent a lot of time in this book telling you what the dangers are, what to avoid, and what will kill your business stone dead. That's because I think you need that information before you start. I could have ignored the problems and told you there was a magic formula that will make you rich, but that wouldn't be fair or useful.

However, having avoided the pitfalls (hopefully in part because you've read this book) there are a lot of good things that will come out of your journey.

For one thing, you'll have a sense of your own worth. You'll be able to wake up in the morning and know why you're going to work. Not just because you need the money, but because you're building something.

You will be able to think up an idea and put it into practice without asking permission. You'll be able to generate a good income year after year just by applying what you know.

So please don't read this book and give up. Read it and start planning. Start working out what you need to do now so that you will be in business for yourself (either as a freelancer on an hourly or daily rate, or running your own show) and make that transition safely.

Have fun.

What's next?

If you'd like to see what other books I've written, you can do that here:

```
amazon.com/author/philcohen
```

Some of what I've written has been fiction (but not this book, honest!) but you'll also find my books on accounting (essential if you're going to start your own business) and B2B selling (essential only if that business is going to sell to other businesses).

If you're about to start your own company, congratulations. I've been running companies for many decades and I can tell you that it's the most fun you can have sitting down.

www.ingramcontent.com/pod-product-compliance
Lightning Source LLC
Chambersburg PA
CBHW071813170526
45167CB00003B/1294